WHISPERS OF THE HEART

CHRISTIE LEIGH BABIRAD

Second Edition.

ISBN: 978-1-963705-87-4

Cover images: Adobestock

Interior images: © Christie Leigh Babirad

Published in the United States of America by Harbor Lane Books, LLC.

www.harborlanebooks.com

Whispers of the Heart is dedicated to my mom, best friend and fellow Sagittarian, Cheryl Suzanne, who shares in my spirit and has always exemplified what it means to keep the spark in oneself alive.

PART ONE—
HEARING YOU

FOR YOU

Welcome to my diary:
A forest of desires.
A riverbed of musings.
Scribed to rouse the soul.

Jazz Soul

Take me downtown to that jazz club you know,
where everyone has a great seat

at the round tables
with the single long-stemmed lush red rose.
This is where spirits like ours take flight,
in the beat,
the saxophone,
the voice scatting away,
going deep
and high
driving us away on a sultry trip,
where everything is more than okay.
Gold-plated and neon-blue,
come as you are in sparkles, bright socks, and cool cat hats.
Hearts grooving with eyes closed,
this is natural.
Falling
into the deliciousness of this life.
There are options in this place.
Freedom.
Creativity.
And a soul I never ever want to leave.

SPRING

It's time to put on that yellow fitted dress.
Smile more.
Realize that big changes aren't always tragic.
Say "yes" to even the passionately short-lived adventures
With the coaxing of the bright golden sun,
The first flower's bloom,
Those red and orange tulips,
White and pink blossoms on the trees,
Forsythias too.
I'm thinking this spring will boldly change everything troubling me,
A season notorious for bringing new life without any pause.

I Remember

Midnight blue velvet skirt,
Three-quartered matching velvet-sleeved top with a summer
sky-blue butterfly in the center.
Cold April night.
The traffic outside my bedroom loud with anticipation as I'm
getting ready.

Whoosh goes the wind—
The cars,
My heart!
Open-toe,
Barely high-heeled silver shoes.
Hair pulled back in a pony-tail,
My guy friend always trying to pull my hair tie out—
The Dawson to my Joey.
Pink and purple lip smackers,
Little black purse,
Paper and a milky pen just in case—
The feather pen wouldn't fit.
Getting out of my mom's car with him.
It's the Middle School Spring Dance.
The cafeteria has been transformed into a dance hall.
Bright blue lights,
A courtyard filled with flowers and small garden trees lit with
yellow bulbs.
The sound system playing loud,
Invigorating my soul all the more.
Whitney Houston,
Mariah Carey,
Janet Jackson,
NSYNC,
Ballads,
R&B,
Pop,
My friend and I separating to make memories of our own.
Looking around for someone who was looking for someone
like me.
And I realized then and now—
I was always different, even when trying to be cool and
fit in.
But the magic seems stronger this way.

The memory is never tied to anyone but my love for
possibility.
And that remains to this day.
I remember who I was,
And who I am now.
I am that same person today,
Full of heart and hope.
And I am happy.

SPECIAL

You've got pieces of me no one else knows,
an edge no one else has seen,
where three in the morning is only for you and me.
How we can be unabashedly honest,
our souls bare to each other?
Must be something really special.

CONCEIVED

If I were to imagine you at this moment you would be staring up at a full silver moon, back against a wall, legs lax on the ground in front of you, arms loose at your side, your body seemingly relaxed, but your heart, your heart beats desperately with passion and questions of how to live in this unmatched-to-your-soul world while feeling that you're running out of time—the same as I.

THESE FEELINGS

Red roses
Taking up much of my mind,
Living for those brightly and passionately lit dance floor
nights,
R&B love songs playing poignantly on the speakers,
The rhythm within me.
The touch of the first summer rays on my neck,
A gentle breeze through my hair,
That look from one soul to another,
Heart beating
Terrified
Knowing that what you're feeling is true love this time,

Forever changed,
Expanded,
Sparkling.
These feelings are at the core of all of us,
Why we are here.

COMMITTED

"I would love to be your guy,"
The sweetest sentiment her soul ever heard.
Bright sneak peek photos slide across her mind.
An early summer sun blazes on the center of her heart.
And she can taste chocolate covered strawberries on her lips.
To be received.
To be desired.
To have someone long to be there for you.
It's like finally being incomparably free.
To know you're quite possibly hugging forever.
Never to be the same again.
Two complete halves, whole.
She dreams this is true.

One Weekend

"I'd settle for one weekend with you."
That's what I said.
Bringing together all these feelings I've been collecting for a
thousand days,

I instinctively knew all along I didn't need to let these vivid
memories go.
Your schedule you cleared.
And my thoughts gravitated toward looking the prettiest
for you.
Rich soil on the breeze the moment I stepped off the plane,
I am now washed in a spirit that authentically matches me like
the perfect date dress.
Being here is like jumping into a lake on a hot summer day,
A sun-lit shimmering waterfall rushing down beside me.
I've been needing this open space,
Quenching my thirst for life.
I didn't realize how dry I had let myself become.
Filled up once again like an hourglass,
If love could be contained.
Excitement building in my chest,
I'm returning to the me I left behind, the moment I left this
beautiful place.
I was so young,
Filled with possibility.
Stepping back as if no time has passed,
But the heart aches with the change of experience.
I'm understanding even more now that we don't have forever
here.
I am in love with this state of being in this exact moment.
Configuring ways to dig deeper roots this time,
I see you walking my way.
You're so different from me.
Yet, everything in me is smiling and singing—
"This is undeniably correct this time."

PLEASE WAKE ME UP

I want to see you tonight.
It's been a long day.

But you know how to stop the passing time.
So, wake me up,
And we will lift into the black star-filled sky.
In your kiss I know we have so much more.
Time is forever in your hold.
In this galaxy all our own,
Where gravity cannot keep us down.
The warm, summer night breeze driving through us,
You take me to this place I need,
Where love really is the priority.
Only the two of us,
Forever.
You awaken me.

Belief

Feeling so overwhelmed,
Feeling so high,

There's a dark blue city night
Behind my eyes,
Taking over my heart
In the powerfully holding daylight,
And I'm no longer in this car
In the summertime,
Firmly planted to the road in a traffic zone.
It's the beginning of Christmastime,
When the Rockefeller Tree is first lit.
We're at a rooftop café
With the bustle of life all around,
Plates clamoring,
Glasses clinking,
And traffic sounding just outside.
A clear new beginning
With a love no longer brand new,
Forever breathtaking it is.
I can see,
With our hands clasped together,
At the center of a candlelit table
Beside a large window,
Looking out.
I absorb,
The first official flight of my life.
That's the way this moment feels,
Under this dark blue city night,
Behind my eyes,
With the traffic zone now ending
And the sun in my rearview, beginning to dim.

7 Days and 7 Nights

She needs a lot of rain right now.
Watching droplets fall from storm clouds above,
She is not angry or sad.
Why the rain represents this she'll never understand.
The looming sun forecasted,
She desires a week of rain.
Continuous,
Clean,
Romantic and magical rain,
Fresh life entering her soul.
A new story is felt in the cool air she breathes,
As Autumn can be seen right around the corner.

What Is Love?

Love Is . . .
Without Limits
Revealing Your Secrets
Unafraid of Consequences
Sacred.

Autumn

The last of the summer days
Coasting into Autumn
Lightning-rimmed clouds
One, the colors of a city when flying above
A dozen shades of blue
Every second there's a change
No less remarkable than the last
Enticingly more as the evening docks
Tasting the cider
Feeling the wind chill every inch of my body
Kissed by an indescribable sense of hope
Overnight color
Everywhere

Making it the perfect time for one of those "nowhere" drives
Nothing but the streetlights
Moonlight and crisp air
The scent of leaves
Invigorating and oh so sweet

In the Sun

A single leaf dances down from a bare branch.
The wind swishes like soft waves rising and falling in the
distance.
A seductive autumn breeze swims luxurious laps across the
cerulean sky.
The warming sun brightly beams overhead.
And a quiet but assured rhythm is set for an eternal track.
On this uniquely blessed November day.

HIDDEN ROMANCE

Twirling around the merits of you.
Running away to secret places;
Seductive hideaways,
The soul doing all of the talking.
Heavenly lit.
Can't be wrong.
This sacred love.
To have and hold.
Where no one other than God knows.

When It Snows

An icy blizzard coats the road ahead
Cancelled plans
A puppy under the covers
Lights out
The scrape of a match for a candle
Cleansing silence
I soak it up and in
Overcome in a feeling of the crisp air entering enclosed places
Everything opens
An ushering in of a fresh start
The finely falling snowflakes
All is new once again

EMOTIONS
RUNNING RED

Red—
Pulsing!
Beating!
Powerfully lingering,
Deeply with a love that can't be defined.
Body tingling with this February snowfall,
These emotions are alive.
Forever reaching beyond the still,
These emotions are key.
With slow dances,
Roses,

A tinkling piano,
The heart taking over the mind.
And I say—What better way to be!
These emotions running red,
Sweetly encompassing all of me.

More Than A Dream

I can picture the entire scene, you know?
I see us in the winter light,
Snow-wet lips on each other.
This heat between us,
we can't believe it's twenty below.
A long-awaited fire

kindles so seductively
between our two hearts.
We meet on the campus where we used to talk
in a hidden spot on a hilltop.
Your kisses reaching down beneath the collar of my red wool
coat,
I almost bite my lip,
thoughts absorbed in this tingling all through me.
I'm lost in all of you.
It's intoxicating
to feel so desired.
I run my hand over your shoulder and chest,
covered up by your light gray jacket.
You place your hand on my waist.
Your light hazel eyes wanting me,
I lock my lips to yours,
permanently slipping away into you.
Feeling our way through these emotions,
so strong,
we inevitably yearn to press beyond the fabric.

WHAT I DON'T SAY

You say you go to bed dreaming of holding me.
What would you say to me telling you I wish the same?
I picture your arm around me as I roll on my side each night.
I trail the imaginings of your body up against mine,
your lips rested on my neck.
These thoughts have me up all night.
I don't tell you though.
Maybe because you are so far away.

These aren't games I play.

This and more would undoubtedly pour from me in just one evening of us being in the same place and time.

What would you say if I told you I never stopped thinking about you?

Even in the years we didn't talk.

Your voice,

your eyes,

your dreams,

your love,

it's all locked in me.

I wonder if you already know.

Inside and Out

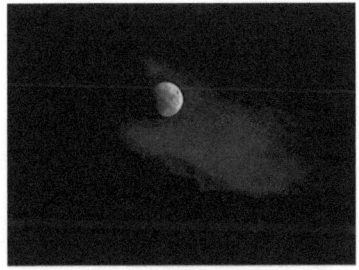

Seems when you wholeheartedly care for someone,
meaning you would drop all acclaim to be at their side,
the way I would with you,
there's a need to know what makes your lover tick
physically,
mentally,
and maybe most importantly,
within their deepest scars.

INFLUENCE

Eyes touch words
strung together with deep intention.

Glistening black ink
at first set on notebook pages.
Such intimate meaning casted out.
Hearts receiving.
Souls touching.
All for the granting of one wish—
To ignite individual inspiration,
higher movement
in reader and author.

What I Want

You want me to be truthful with you?
I want to fly with you without a fear of crashing.
I want you to take my hand.
I want a safe landing, a place to come home to,
only to take-off for the deep blue once again.
I want all my adventures with you.

High on your every touch.
Uninhibited.
Free.
The electric strings playing us always into something new.
There are grand mountaintops to experience.
Fields of flowers to lay back in.
I want everything with you.
I want to be forever impassioned,
and done with all that doesn't echo your sexy-sweet,
long-held,
kiss!

Scarlet Secrets

You might uncover these secrets in my poetry.
Maybe you'll find them in close time spent within this garden
of deep love I've been trying to grow.
Here live the people and places I try to take with me wherever
I go.
You'll often find me wearing Scarlet Red,

From my dress to the flush in my cheeks
To my truest spirit I tend to wear candidly open.
Sometimes this is of course a mistake.
Sipping on a Passion Colada in a music club.
In the tiny nook of the bustling city pub.
At the small candle-lit table with the bright local or imported
flower—
Always unique,
Always elegantly exotic,
Usually a deep purple or strawberry red.
You'll find me in early a.m. drives through the village to see the
Christmas lights.
Within chilly nights.
In a slow dance embrace where the whole world disappears,
You on the last chorus kissing me with a "let's go home"
whisper in my ear.
It's within these moments that all of my Scarlet Secrets are
revealed,
The most intimate and soulfully free places within me that I
hold so profoundly dear.

Farewell to All These Cards I Hold

Let's be honest,
I'm becoming quite weary holding these cards so close to my
body.
Pretending I don't need that certain somebody.
Hiding the "Single."
Hiding how badly I yearn to change this status.
Not for the likes.
Only for this last key puzzle piece,
Longed for since the middle school dance floor.
Seems everyone else is set for The Ark.
Finding someone can't be that difficult.
But I'm not waiting on simply someone.

A young girl doesn't dream for that.
I can't betray her now.
Still a part of me.
Forever me.
I'm looking for "the one."
Don't even think about calling me unrealistic!
I've waited too long to allow this deep wish to fly away.
I'm telling you honestly from my soul,
I desire someone who encourages my every goal.
An unconditional and unforgettable love,
Challenging me to become everything in my heart.
I've finally figured out what I want,
A partner in this increasingly crazy life.
I'm laying these dreams all out here.
I don't care who sees.
All the tv couple music videos I've spent countless evenings pining over,
The daily romance I desire,
A mix of a Dawson Leery and a Dylan McKay could be my beau.
I smile.
I think he could be.
Wherever you may be, won't you please come and find me.
Tonight, I'm saying farewell to all these cards I hold.

AFTER THE FIRST ENCOUNTER

Deep blue I walk into
Orange runs left to right
Right to left
Up and down
Down and up
Throughout the body

In a flurry of motion
Yet I am nonetheless convinced
All directions lead to the heart
And I am paralyzed
To put the adrenaline out
Only a song will do
The perfect track to encapsulate the first encounter
But once the melody spreads
Like the scent of lavender often heals
The real trouble begins

READING

I always feel better when reading those stories that belong to Love. There is no greater means to slip through the mind's walls than to be fully absorbed in a good story.

FUTURE CASTING

She's tossing out her line these days,
Into the immense ocean of life,
Wondering what will be caught,
Most likely in the nick of time.
She doesn't know if the stories are for her.
A man whose deep love for her feels granted from Heaven
above.
A nursery with two sweet girls or a boy.
As time ticks quickly onward
She stands waiting and wondering,
What move will bring her closer to the mystical fortune teller,
The reveal of what is meant to be?

TEMPORARY

I still think about you
And the way we used to talk.
You slipped to the back of my mind for a while.
I was foolish to think I had been cured of you.
Only took the voice of an artist who reminds me of you,
Singing on my radio tonight.
There's no doubt you would have been my guy,
At least for a little while.
There were many differences between us,
But where it counts, we were a perfect match.
I still continue to want you.
Staying up late till I was ready to fall asleep,

Checking in with me in the day because you missed me too.
For me, we were as intimate as if we were in the same place at
the same time.
Maybe that's difficult to understand,
But where my heart went makes this statement true as can be.
This is the stuff that can't be created with sex.
How would I know?
It's your being with my being I still think about often before I
go to bed at night.
You've been with others, I know, but you keep coming back to
me too.
This is not in my imagination, is it?
Something undeniably special happened between us.
We always seem to be temporary for each other,
Coming in and out of each other's lives
In cycles.
And yet, you inspire so many of these writings of mine.
Dear God, I pray the right man comes my way,
But you will always be undeniable for me.
I truly believe you will forever have a place in my soul.
And there's nothing temporary about that!

THE WEIGHT OF LOVE

These arms of hers haven't been given their weight just yet.
One wrapped around her,
The other at her side.
She sleeps alone with all her delayed dreams,
Waiting on the day she will collide with him and know.
She carries a strength to show a deep love,

A healing touch that sweetly burns.
These arms for him will be irreplaceable.
He will know he has never been valued this strongly.
Taking all his deepest worries away,
Her arms will be given their weight,
Never again to be wrapped around herself alone.

BRIGID

Irish Goddess of Poets,
My fickle muse of writing
Only floats in with raw truth,
Careless of my doubts.

PART TWO—
SCATTING AWAY

SIGNALS

He leans in.
Stopped!
In this one sweet place and time.
Her heart races.
Eyes search for trouble.
Electric emotions like currents beat.
Neither able to resist this passionate heat.
Two souls in this moment pulled together,
Meant to connect,
Beyond the warning signals.
Caution ahead!

Inner Attack

She gets wound up
in a cyclone of lines.

Imperfection she finds,
an insecurity that binds.

She untangles
in a rainstorm of fear.
"Time waits for no one, my dear."
She wipes hard at that first tear.

She surrenders
in a sunshine field of grace.
Love takes insecurity's place,
her knowing deeply it is only the heart she must face.

Jealousy

I think it might be a little jealousy taking its toll on me.

I see you swinging your hips as you sing on that brick back-
drop stage.
You're starting out on a dream I've been dreaming on,
Smiling the I've-made-it smile.
I play the video over and over again,
Inspired in my hole.
Oh, how I wish I could dig myself out!
Insecurity with a mix of fear,
One lethal combination.
You're confident and I want to be too.
At times I know I have it.
Feeling like I'm running out of time.
Not knowing how to take the next step.
I wish you could tell me.
It drives me crazy watching you.
I have to tell you,
You strike me as the kind of girl who never got shattered,
Everything always falling into place.
Don't think I don't realize that I could be all wrong
about you.
I'm starting to think jealousy has its hold on me,
Poisonous in every way.
I listen to you again.
I know it's not as difficult as I'm making it out to be.
Letting my tears of uncertainty wash away,
Letting the jealousy go and any forward move to be made.
I have a fire blazing in my heart,
Making me know for sure that this desire is right,
That it's worth more than my fears.
Bringing myself out of the hole I put myself in,
All soul on that stage,
That's what I'm going to do.
Very soon I'll be smiling that I've-made-it smile just like you.

And I can't help but thank you for being my inspiration.
Thank you for making me so jealous of you.

In A Perfect World

In a perfect world you would be home with her this Christmas
To start again.
A perfect duet you two could be,
And your unique dreams would strengthen together.
You wouldn't have to be alone with your best friend by your
side,

In a perfect world nothing would have changed.
You could go driving around with her to see all the fancy
homes decorated with extravagant lights,
Or take a trip into the city to see a show,
Side by side falling asleep on your shoulder on the train ride
home.
And when the monsters came up again you could take it to the
boardwalk like you used to,
No matter the weather,
You could have each other back again
This Christmas into The New Year
In a perfect world.

Set Me Free

I find my haven here,
between the words
that give my heart their wings,
away from the permeating darkness he brings.

You Remain

If I briefly stepped left with you.
Maybe if I had held your hand tighter.
Just maybe then my feelings would have moved to you.
And you would have instantaneously turned around.
But I heard you can't change the way the river runs.

Whoever said this first couldn't have been struck the way
I was,
To be so cavalier.
I still reminisce in the silence,
When we matched in rhythm,
Stepping into the same beat every time.
Strings of possibility were a constant in the sparkle of your
deep brown eyes.
And still when I hear a duet,
There's not a second when I don't think
That could be us.
Like it was
In the backseat of that shiny dark blue Oldsmobile.
My friend,
There's just no moving past you.
There's no amount of time that could heal your departure
from my life.
I guess you've just become a stone in the bitter
This earthly place doles out from time to time.
I will still dance.
I will still laugh.
I will fall in love.
But I know enough,
After almost fifteen years,
You will remain.
Not like that birthmark you learn to love.
Nor compared to the beautiful light seen when perspectives
have been changed.
No.
You exist in the broken pieces
I've learned to gently live with.

Thank You, Lord

Thank you for him, Dear Lord.
When hatred spews outside my door
Louder and louder
With no end in sight
Night after night,
I remember that you blessed me with him,
A glowing light
Burning bright
Reminding me that this is not right.
My heart then settles,
And my thoughts travel to his love.

Oh, thank you Lord for him,
A promise of better tomorrows.

Some Days

Some days I feel I have nothing left to give anyone.
There's tightness in my chest as I let the fires burn around me.
"You can't save him" is the internal line on repeat.
My eyes close and I try to bring my attention to the safe place
of love,
As I say goodnight to the sun.

WITNESS TO HOPE

They locked in an embrace dispelling a history of goodbyes.

Thick smoky strands of golden filled the girl's deeply
empathetic,
Already-weighted heart.
Overwhelmed this girl was of the elder's darkness,
But also enthralled by the simultaneous contradiction playing.
Where pain was obvious, so was the woman's incandescently
passionate,
Almost fury-like
Light.
In this connected embrace,
The woman let this young girl in on the secret,
The strength one can always hold.
The soul never betrays itself,
Living deep inside the heart for the repeated reclaiming
Of everything you were always meant to be.

Poison Apple

Thank you for this ache deep in the pit of my soul.
This is the only remnant.
I am still baffled by your game
twice played.
You gave me a rotten apple
that shined bright red and new on the outside.

So foolish I was.
We were a false love from the start.
I did know.
But I let you in anyway.
And with a quick snap of my heart,
you were on your way once again.
You never did have trouble letting people go.
If anyone dared to disagree with you,
in an instant it was friend to foe.
We're literally hundreds of miles apart.
That's why I ultimately thank you.
You made me see,
so genuinely,
not sarcastically,
and not even in anger anymore.
I feel the magic coursing through my veins again.
You helped me work again.
This is how I create.
When given a poisonous apple,
extraordinary hurt turns into masterpieces for me.
An artist,
I will forever be.
Once again, I am on the verge of making expanded dreams
come true.
I give you a standing ovation.
Because of you,
I will achieve more.
Because of you,
I am unblocked,
always telling the world I am far from self-made.

To You

You left right before the dedication.
Some may say this to be in perfect timing.

I can't agree.

Time, I long to erase in regard to you.

The hurt has run deep into the place where memories stay.

Your imprint I guarantee will be recalled when I'm old and gray.

I may not remember your name,

but you,

yeah, you somehow will remain.

That's why no relief can come

from a sentence taken away on a typewritten page.

To you I was a chapter.

To me you were a book I wish I hadn't been so determined to finish,

each chapter more bitter than the last.

Though,

like most books,

I guess I learned a lot.

BURNED

She understands the diagnosis now.
You were "burned," she was told, matter of fact,
Like this would be easy to treat now.
The fire started with the slickest fingers on the match.
She can still hear the scrape.
One swipe is all it took,
Set on the center of this thin-skinned heart where such trust
and vivid memories lie.
They're all lies,
These many books this "friend" filled.

She understands the diagnosis now.

You were "burned," her true friends explain,
over and over again,
like this is treatable now.
But what do you do when you still feel the sting?
She keeps asking, "*why?*"
"*Why do these ones who repeatedly hurt get to just skip away?*"
She's not this one's first victim, after all.
"*Why is there no holding on for them, no guilt for the pain they caused?*"

All she can say,
If she had the choice of a superpower,
it would be forced care.
She would have those people sit in the fire they lit,
until they wholeheartedly understand,
it's heartless to treat another this way.

THE EDIT

Within her soul
There are many songs

Yearning to be released.
Housed in the chambers of her heart,
Where life's strength flows,
There are chapters never printed.
The past, seemingly unfulfilled,
Tipping the scales for the future
She fears.
So, she travels through time for clarity.
In pages past she sees
A young preteen girl
Spending too many days quiet,
Staying out of the way,
Her voice cracking when she hits the stage.
She thinks she's not pretty.
She wishes for one of the "cool boys" to ask her to the school dance,
And travel down the lazy river with her hand in his.
Then there's the teenager
With all those same wishes
Rushing down a slide this time,
Faster this time.
She sometimes sees herself
Pretty.
But the "cool boy" is still the same,
And she's beginning to see,
He's only looking for one thing,
The quick and instant
In false love
Not the adventure or romance she seeks.
The young woman in her twenties,
Was filled with voices contradicting her own,
Running with abandon in her mind,
But she stayed the course.
She spent mostly isolated years scribbling lines in her book,

Pasting true pictures to her within this chamber.
The "cool boy" had married another,
Though the alone time changed her,
No longer was she interested in what he had to offer.
Now, in her thirties,
She sees herself mighty!
She sees herself as exquisite
Within all of her scars.
The "cool boy" she longs for is much different now.
He's a man,
And he echoes every part of her,
Loving every piece of her.
And she is ready
Like never before
To experience everything,
All that would have been superficial had they come at the time
she wanted.
The scales did in fact tip,
The edits finding their way in through additions,
But never any deletions.
The book bound and out to the world,
The next part of her story is only just beginning.
She realizes, with going back in her memories,
She is fearful no more,
And beyond ready for that stage!

Earth and Fire

Even in title I put you before me.
Baby, you got me good!
It's no wonder I had to pay the fee.

You had a required ground.
I needed your unconditional love.
Seems I was always freedom-bound.

Lack of trust was our end.
You thought I didn't truly want you.
Neither of us was willing to bend.

I lived for the future I could see,
from one soul-stirring conversation to the next,
looking for you to wait a little for the heart of me.

Off the Script

I would have called you tonight.
My spirit was lit like a Broadway Number.
An over-decade success.
You were my mentor,
as I was an understudy in the background chorus.
But fate had an unscripted swan song,

and a pre-cursor plot twist,
I could have never predicted.
The one I revered the most,
showed his pride for me was a hoax,
as I was cast the main player in my first show.

You Only Live Once

"You only live once," he reminded her.

However, this fact has never diminished strength in her mind.
What gives her pause, is her love is a love that will bind.
When she falls, she does so like no other of her kind.
Given to one who wavers, her spirit will assuredly take long to again find.

YOUR TIME

Awakening each day, the same.
My eyes open to one dull notch,
Never wide in wonder these days.
Hope—is a signal I can't seem to reach.
Continually startled by reality.
Shocked into acceptance.
Like a clapboard to the chest.
I reflect . . .
Am I still here?
This dull ache has become my normal since you left.
You flew away too soon,

Too young,
Never minding my visions of starry skies and velvet gowns,
Legends and all these mountains I thought we'd climb.
The time we had was too short.
I feel . . .
Cheated!
All the memories we were given,
They were minimal to the dreams I had.
But all the people chime,
"It must have been your time."

WHERE YOU ARE

I miss you.

In lesser moments I demand that you know what you've done
to me.
I haven't been the same since you left.
You filled my imagination with Sapphire Stars and Scarlet Red
Romance.
Now there's only this black night.
I can't escape.
I struggle to see the daylight.
Since you flew away,
This pain speaks in mumbling undertones.
This pain envelops me,
Reiterating smugly,
There's something missing.
I can never have the magic of you and me back again.
But I know you.
From Heaven,
You must have a plan.
A perfect synchronicity.
A splash of serendipity.
When I least expect you to,
You'll be ready to surprise me in only the way you could.
You'll let me know,
You miss me too.
You are still with me.
This is only a different mode,
Not a single song less joyful than the ones you sang to me on
my birthday each year.

FRUSTRATION

She's so sick of being lonely.
Impulses begging!
Soul raging!
But she doesn't want to be left with only a memory.
Pulling out the weeds,
Trying not to look,
To play on repeat sweet moments of ecstasy,
The true pieces of love.
Knowing that in reality it is all gone.
Knowing when acting from frustration,
There's no way they could last.

PUSHED BACK TEARS

What is the cost of the tears he doesn't shed? *"I've seen him cry before."* I said this as if it was akin to spotting an owl in the daylight. I told him he could tell me anything. But in his on-the-edge eyes, he doubted this well-intentioned sentiment of mine. *"How can I?"* he seemed to ask me. *"I see the way your body tenses and your lips force themselves closed when my eyes begin to well up and my face turns red."* *"It's only because I rarely see this emotion from you. It's startling."* *"So, you admit it, you see?"* He swallows the pain down. All these boys taught to be tough, growing into men with broken hearts. The cost of all these pushed back tears for our brief feeling of security can't be worth the loss of their powerful spirit and the strength in their hands that touch a woman's soul like nothing else. Something needs to change in us ladies to allow these pushed back tears to be set free.

Cycles

Is this it?
We went through us a second time.

Ending the same as we did last time.
I was left strung on the same hope,
We could have changed together.
We could have figured a way to hang on in a different way,
With a little less pain than yesterday.
Is this it?
We surely couldn't repeat this cycle a third time.
It's either goodbye forever,
Or, a surprise some day.

STRONGER THAN YOU THINK

I'm stronger than you think.
I could have handled the up and down of your love.
Did you justify your dismissal with *I deserve better?*
Baby, I do.
But I still wanted to love you.
I could have handled the swing,
The times you'd need to push off without me.
You thinking you did us a favor by cutting the string,
That's what holds the greatest sting.
But I can handle you being gone again too.
I only wish you could have stayed to see,
My love is far stronger than you think.

A Heart's Restart

How many hearts have we left cracked at the end of our days?
How many hurtful statements have we made in the name of
retaliated pain?
Tonight, I make a wish to change the score,
To begin again by loving more.
I wish for a middle ground to be found forevermore.

Closed Book

You said you wanted to know more about me.
I could tell you anything.
I could ask you anything.
You left the moment I began.
Only receiving the inside flap blurb,
You wanted to solve the problem.
I wanted you to already see,
Strength and Breathtaking Beauty,
Like red tulips drying in a sunlit field,
Unbelievably flourishing from the storms the night before,
Like a precious miracle,
The way I felt when I first met you.

I wanted you to encourage me with the most genuine love to
share more,
One page at a time.
For the first time I wanted to open this closed book of mine.
I wanted to reveal to you all these secrets, opening myself
completely to you.

WIDE OPEN HEART

She has left every door open,
Wide open.
Every window,
Every way you could come into her,
Wide open.
Wishing only for the last talk to be deleted.
Nothing holding your hearts back anymore.
Nothing holding her back anymore.
Like the intimate glow of a warm sun shining overhead,
You both know that what you had was true.
You must know she loves you too.

Now only needing you to make the first move,
Reassuring her once more it's she you have wanted all along.

.

BROKEN DOWN

She wishes for a place to run away to,
to stay forever if she chooses to,
to begin completely anew,
away from the depression daggers he throws with such force.
Stabbed with the first toss,
the wound is a black hole,
suctioning her down so she will always feel a bit of the
impression.
Piercing to the point where there will always be damage,
to the point where she can't summon any care
anymore.

She no longer wishes for the man if this will all be a variation
of the same.
Her belief has waned tonight.
She only wants her little dog.
Forevermore.
She will help create the rest of her life on her own.

No One Cared
for You More

Brandy burning
down into the pit of my stomach.
No one cared for you more.
No one fought for you more.
I let the hurt go time and time again,
Yet realizing deep that the message had to come from
somewhere.
With fluidity the poison was cast from your loose lips,
Somewhere within this had to be your truth,
What you really think of me.

Mantra

I gave more than I received.
You're not any loss to me.
I must remember.

FATE

God knew,
I wasn't to share my deepest secrets with you.
Secrets are precious jewels,
No matter the truths they possess.
These essential pieces in my autobiography,
I stopped concerning my heart with the uncovering long ago.
Now I have greater self-respect keeping me from sharing these
moments with you.
The between the lines,
Stories told,
They would have you sacredly belonging to me.
The first to know.

The first to keep.
You were never meant to know me that deep.
God knew,
You weren't the one.
Manifested through uncertainty in my soul,
I was stopped every time,
No matter how determined I fell into the illusion of how I
wanted us to go.
God knows the someone out there for me,
The one I will spill every secret to.
Precious jewels shining between these hearts,
I'll witness how God was pulling these strings of fate all along.

Weak Moment

She slips back under his tender voice repeating a past line held close.

He slides into the enclaves of her memory,
Sweet with casual intent.
She pushes back with reminders of their ending,
Stings of a dozen slow farewells.
She thought this door she had double locked.
He trails her heart with love that was unequivocally true.
And she sinks into these pieces of their story,
Absorbing what she wishes was whole.
But she is alone.
And she resolves,
Soon,
She will need to accept reality
Over the moment of weakness
She indulged,
As he goes
Silent.

THE ME YOU SEE

The me you see is still a girl,
She's not quite a woman,
Missing the experiences that have shaped me.
I don't believe you see.
It's ludicrous the way you dismiss me,
When I know
So simply
How to take care of your every need.
Realities no one should ever have to accept, I did,

Only to build my heart right back up
Over and over again,
So many times.
You have no idea.
You only see this sweet girl before you,
Wearing a flowered dress,
Her cheeks flushed,
And a smile on her face,
Like she has seen nothing at all,
Like she doesn't know the superficiality you're without a
doubt coming from.

LIFE LINE

I would have called more.
Slights, I would have simply let be.
Fears of being hurt wouldn't have stopped me.
I would have bought that one-way ticket.
If I had known you were to leave us young,
I would have saved every voice message.
I would have never taken your presence like the wind.
I would have held onto you,
like my favorite shirt worn only in the most tender
summertime,
under the brightest crescent moon.

To Rekindle

I played our song over and over again.
I could place the needle with my eyes closed,
Until the track began to skip,
The scratches began to show.
I think this may be how love goes.
When you play the original song,
No matter how the music's notes once spoke like magic to
both hearts,
The fire fades with the wind that blows,
Only to be rekindled with the remix from that same old soul.

How Much Longer?

How much longer must she wait?
She caught a glimpse of you late last night,
A bright light,
A mere flashbulb of a moment,
And then you were gone.
Never before has she felt
How very much she wants you.
There's an essential place in her soul only you can fill.
In a world so cataclysmically superficial,
Where not even extremes awaken most for very long—
With you she only sees the truest love,
Someone who deeply cares.
With you she sees the incredible!

She sees endlessly passionate days
She couldn't have imagined in her wildest dreams.
She sees Deeply Colored Sunsets with you,
Crashing Water,
Hot Days,
Cool Nights;
A Cotton Candy Colored Kind of Love.
Your strong arms wrapped around her,
Holding her close to your body,
She knows that you are meant for her.
She is meant for you.
She can feel you, as real as can be.
All she wants to know is—
How much longer must she wait?

Unwelcomed Secrets

Secrets given second-hand accounts,
She knows she'll eventually have to turn over those stones,
On her own
The burdens she let others carry,
Few questions she asked,
She will have to absorb the stories for protection they told,
Revealing the raw and bitter truth this time.
A reality she knows will bombard her with emotion she has
never felt,
To move forward
Maybe stronger
Maybe with more grace

These truths she now has to possess
No longer shielded.
She will have to find a place within to tuck them away,
By herself
Where she can carry these secrets with peace and resolution
For all the rest of her earthly days.

A Failure,
You Are Not!

Come back home my friend.
Leave the turncoats and dark spirits.
The sun in you knows.

Hurricane

Our relationship was like a storm drill siren
Getting ready for a hurricane soon coming our way

West to East.
Together, we boarded the windows of the past we wanted to
keep,
Aware they would not be able to withstand the storms.
We thought,
I thought,
Together we held a strength greater than anything before,
But when the hurricane came—
Like all storms of this magnitude—
Everything built seemed foolish.
Our relationship was like a storm drill,
Practical on paper,
Meaning relatively nothing when the storm actually came.
Understanding shifted to self-preservation,
You snuck out at midnight,
Sliding into your shiny black Lexus.
You headed South
But after the storm, a rose bush I planted alone in the corner
of the yard
Bloomed
The brightest red,
A passionate scarlet red,
And I realized
I don't need anyone for these storms.
I made it through with my faith and all-feeling soul alone.

My Place

Today I want to lose the day,
The troubles and harsh light placed on me,
Alone in this room.
Let the day turn into night,
Slowly in romantic turns,
Intently driven,
Naturally moving.
Beach doors reflect beams of spirit,
I believe,
I feel these sparks
In different places inside me,
With my arms way up in the air

I dream that I can soar.
No one can come in and try to control me here.
They can seek,
But they won't find.
I freely go in and out of the places the song takes me,
Saying what I have needed so desperately to say,
Seeing what kept the anger inside for such a long time,
Pulling out the whole story now,
The pretty
And the painfully unsettling,
In this place alone,
My place,
Where I can let it all out.
That's exactly what I'm going to do,
Today into tonight.
I'm going to dance all the way through.

My Fellow Woman

I saw the story on the news.
You commented—
"Why, oh why, did this lady refuse to speak up sooner?"
Heat filled my face.
My heart was beating like a drum in a parade.
I wanted to clap back.
I wanted to say . . .
something.
But I knew my voice would be drowned by the masses.
This is the exact answer to "*why?*"
It's because of you, partially.
I'd actually give you more than half the credit.

My Fellow Woman.
I myself have "spoken up,"
with your kind in reply,
"Oh, that's just the way he is."
You'd say this with a gentle chuckle,
a sip of wine on the country club patio.
Or, *"It's just a cultural difference."*
"It's not anything to make anything of."
Let me please just say this:
People often speak up when they feel they will be heard,
when they have more power in numbers,
or they express their feelings in poetry and art like me.
People often speak up when they're at peace,
financially secure,
like most of you who would pose such callous questions.

Dear Gentlemen

This poem is for you.
I see you,

but I know your voice has been silenced.
You must know how greatly you matter to us,
the women who witness the truth of the matter.
My heart is clear,
and its beat tells me the truth aching to be told.
Media likes to lump you all as one,
keeping matters simple,
making situations extreme in consequence and hurt.
But this outcry is solely directed at the many who received
their "welcome to the club cards" prior to conception.
They are arrogant and entitled.
You couldn't dream of entering their wealth through anything
but passionate creativity,
hard work,
open intelligence,
and lots and lots of hustle!
Yet, you've been herded with them.
But not hired like them.
They hold the high positions,
but smile as they preach inclusion.
They say women make the best lawyers,
but would never let go of their position in place of a woman or
anyone else.
They are so comfortable!
They have so much to say.
They are loud,
choosing to live in a far-from-inclusive way.
But I believe—
The New Age Is Coming!
Some of these individuals have finally been caught,
and their deeds are starting to become mainstream knowledge
in Pop Music and Movements.
You've never belonged with them.
My Gentle Man,

You stand with a pure heart,
whether from privilege or not.
And you are the first to protect.
I know this.
We as women need you.
You were never the ones to push us aside,
for all of time.

THE MILLENNIALS

You call us the "Me-Generation"—
Labeling us self-centered and entitled.
You look to the now, mournfully,

And back with such reverence.
But you were the teachers,
And we were the students.
You turned us away,
And taught us to fight.
We started working our way up,
And you rewarded the moment's novelty.
You preached diversity,
And showed us nepotism.
You said that without a formal education you can't expect much,
So, we shelled out dozens of bills,
You proceed to tell us that with all of the education, we should take what we can get.
Then you sit us down and look at our resumes with a frown and tell us we have no related experience.
So, you see—
For the "Me-Generation" to have happened,
It took much encouragement by you.
Through the hypocrisy we witnessed,
And the beating down that was marshaled by you,
We were simply the students—
You were our teachers.

Heavy Heart

Choked up by the smallest triggers.
Books are stored atop suitcases.
Won't be going anywhere for a while.
The future is a new unknown.
The masked people visibly show the horror movies I always
stayed away from.

So many bright eyes
seem
unfazed by all these changes.
Old lovers continue to hold grudges.
And all I want is to fall in love,
to sink deeply into a pool of this absorbing truth
nothing else penetrating into my soul.
I wish for my heavy heart to melt away,
once
and for all.

PERMANENT

I don't believe I'll ever be able to erase
That expression on your face.
You didn't want to see me
On your doorstep.
The storybook notion
I built my life's purpose upon,
Taken away,
And you didn't even know
It's okay.
I can't pretend that I hadn't wanted you to stay,
But I don't need you to come back anymore.
We belong to different galaxies,

But still you once belonged to mine
And thirteen years sometimes has a way of staying with you, I
guess.
Like a single star in the sky,
You are
In my mind shining,
The same here as you are there,
The same now as you were then.
Despite all that has been tainted and hurt,
You belong as a piece that is permanent in me.

ALL I WANT

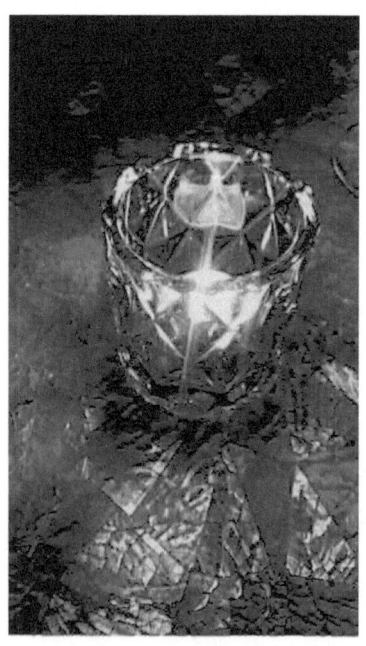

What if I screamed?
What if I let all the pain out in this foreign place?

So much darkness—
Surrounded by bright walls, tables, and chairs—
It's such a contradiction.
Tired of feeling low with no view ahead—
I feel as if I have no control.
Writing by flashlight tonight—
There are signs, but the order is nowhere near.
Worn from those who see less of me—
A little kindness and belief is what I need.
Life is terrible when this becomes difficult to find.
When no one can see.
Silently here,
I'm praying for tomorrow to change.
It's all I want.

A Love Story Lesson

This is a love story that has no root.
Any sort of reasoning is moot.

A tale of "Don't let this happen to you!"
Wearing a scarlet red disguise.
Clouding any ambition to rise.
Ending with the grays that never turn over to clear.
It's a message of warning,
To cease labeling the loyal as boring.
For the loyal are the ones who wear no disguise.
And they happen to be the loves who will continually want
you to rise.

No One Knows

No one knows
These secrets
She holds,
Wrapped around her like a snake,
Slithering around tighter and tighter it goes,
Rough scales of seductive emerald and gold,

Yet she pretends she is free,
Continually drawing out droplets of inner strength and
ambition
To create an endlessly flowing stream
To quiet the hissing,
To save herself while simultaneously fighting to rescue him.
No one knows,
They only see selfless sweetness and love,
They have no idea how tightly she is wound.

A Toxic Mind

How do you save someone who doesn't want to be saved?
When remarks are thrown like a continuous shotput of sticks
and stones,
The heartbreak is guaranteed to be greater than any broken
bones.
So how do you let the hurt roll off your shoulders?
When each breakdown cuts in a different way,
Each time creatively deeper,
Into the memory these episodes will forever stay.
And how can you stand by and watch—
A once-bright being in mental anguish fade away?
But how can you leave—

When prayers continue for them to reach out for the help they so desperately need.

COME JULY

I'm trying to embrace the new season,
but the spring has a way of teasin'.
Bright colors on the people and trees,
but the scent of funeral lilies has a way of creeping in and
bringing me to my knees.
I wish I could embrace the season most others love.

The colors are truly from Heaven above.
I wish I could put on a pastel-shaded dress,
and not feel society's persistence putting me to the test.
Maybe it's planetary, too much water dousing my fire,
too much of the earth grounding me down further,
but spring seems to always have a way of causing me to tire.
That's why, to the Yellow, Kelly Green, Teal Blue, and Cotton
Candy Pink,
I must for now say goodbye.
I guess it's inevitable that I'll have to say, that I will see the
world again in July.

INCONCEIVABLE

How do I appreciate you
when lies
and the cruelest personal truths you tell?

How do I respect you
when I know how you've cheated
the one person as close to an angel as one can be?

And how do I even tolerate you
when I know you don't care about anyone at all?

You care only for yourself.

The purpose of you being in our lives is—
Inconceivable.

DIFFERENT

Trapped on this playground of seesaws.
Figures I'd be the only one stuck as high as they can go.

It's uneasy never feeling a sense of steady ground.
A fool at times.
I sometimes wish to be happy here.
But I'm way up high,
In a broken place,
A heart incomplete,
Without a ray of sunlight shining down anywhere in sight.

CHRISTMAS THIS YEAR

Don't tell me another Christmas season is going to go by
without you again.
Don't tell me it's going to be another everyday airport scene.
Everybody with somebody but me.
The reason I alone only boarded the plane once.
Something I never want to experience again.
Couples.
Hand in hand.
Side by side.
Everyone with somebody but me.
Now Thanksgiving is near.
Santa will be showing up on Macy's sleigh.
And I want you badly,

More and more each day.
Yes, I am complete without you.
I don't need a rescue.
But I need you,
That soul connection,
The intimate tie that no other relationship can supply.
The cold air chills every bit of bare skin.
The snow begins to fall.
The looks become softer with me wearing sweaters and hats
my grandma made.
The heart becomes warmer.
And desire becomes richer in color and feeling.
Everywhere it's red, silver, and gold.
This is the season that centers love.
It's the season that makes everyone want to get closer.
The lonely stick out as the music calls everyone to feel alive.
Without you it's only another year.
More than ever, I need you with me.
Under the mistletoe we could sweetly be.
Christmas this year could be the first of forever with you,
Your hand in my hand,
Us side by side.

SECOND CHANCES

I didn't think I ever took anything for granted,
But looking at these pictures
I'm beginning to think differently.

With my mind of the past
Having often wandered to the missing parts.

What a fool I was.

I didn't think seeing my favorite artists live with my mom
would end so soon,
With a pandemic and violence worldwide taking center stage.
It has all got me feeling blue.

I know I should be happy to have lived these experiences at all.
And I truly am.
But if given second chances,
I promise to do everything in my power to be as present as
can be.
The way I live my life now,
Every day,
Complete.

Cloud Cover

Emanating the energy of a developing storm,
The smoke fills every room like a fire that always starts off
small.
Methodically targeting the hearts of everyone in its path,
There's a desperate race to get far away fast,
Before one's inner strength is unable to last.

Blocked

Sometimes the mind can effectively knock you down.
You allow your blind faith to lapse.
You chalk your past hope up to being young,
Not knowing better,
While still calling up that girl you were.
You know that she is the one who can save you.
And she will.

Time and time again.
With a little sleep on it,
A little of the right song—
The one that always makes you feel everything,
And the purest love from the Jack Russell at your side.

BETTER THAN THERAPY

Twirling around my discontent with an open notebook on my lap and pen in my right hand.

Finding different ways to relay my many emotions.
Envisioning the co-stars with me reading my lines at times,
thinking—
"Wow, I had no idea I hurt her so badly!"
"I can't believe she compared me to a snake and a poisoned
apple. We're done for sure now!"
And on the happier side of the street,
"I'm touched that what we had meant so much to her."
No matter the situation,
Writing is often my way of saying goodbye to thoughts that
have taken up long residencies in my mind.
I play with lines, words, and metaphors that bring me to the
other side,
All with a wish that I have brought a crowd of people with me,
Everyone released through the healing I try to break through
to, when I write in this undeniably personal way.

In Medias Res

The wind carries a winter chill still,
But the air carries the scent of spring.

Garbage is scattered along the thinly grass-lined parkway,
But a brighter place is intimated in the lone scarlet tulip rising
up from the ground.
There aren't letters or phone calls coming in.
There's nothing out of the ordinary in my day.
I'm solitarily running on a feeling,
But for the first time this feeling stays.
I'm apparently in medias res.

Often when you're in medias res, in between happenings, you
need to go back before going forward, remembering not only
the difficult times, but the beautifully unique-to-your-life
memories that can never be tainted or taken away.

TEARS FALL

Tears fall with the birth of a new awakening,
For the story that no longer remains,
And the reveal that has yet to be shown.
Tears fall for the impatient pain that is entirely felt,
When the energy is at its maximum, yet the heart is required to
be still,
The soul wanting nothing more than to be free.
Tears fall for the once-in-a-lifetime shift meant to fill your new
story with great light.
Tears fall for every dream coming true,
All at once.

A MUSICAL GIRL

She saw her first musical young, sitting in a high school auditorium. She watched who she viewed as adults, one step away from Broadway, sing powerfully with grand personalities, a soundtrack story of love and passion. Inside her, this young girl remains—awakened—and to this day she is still enlivened with the spirit of these shows. In writing and one day singing somewhere, she is committed to making this untold dream and early influence take hold.

Part Three—
The Spotlight

FOREVER DESIRE

I never want this feeling to go away.
Head nodding with the tap of the drum
in this song
playing through these headphones.
Feeling the soulful trail of this melody
in my heart,
in my mind,
in my body.
I never want to lose this magic.
It has me anxious,
waiting on you to get home tonight,
to get cozy with you,

Spirited thoughts swirling in my mind.
I picture my hand feeling its way
over the muscle of your arm
to your heart.
Our eyes connecting,
I feel your hands on my hips.
I'm anew every time you touch me.
I melt into you with each passionate beat.
And I never want to stop needing this.
Lips sealing in this matchless kiss,
In your arms I'm always consumed,
overwhelmed,
in love.
And I always want to be,
in this forever desire,
attached to only you.

Autumn Light

Shining through shedding trees
over rooftops
within the blending of a sultry dusty and bright blue sky,
fluffy white clouds filled with your beams,
decorate
where we look to Heaven.
And your light—
Your light has my heart
pumping passion again,
with one romantic excursion after another
coming like dancing daydreams,
inevitably taking my soul

off on a rocket ship to the crisp salt air,
to the now-deserted island beach
as I feel wonderfully
like a castaway,
but deeply believing,
one incomparable sweater embrace
will soon be coming my way.

Winter Love

These songs are playing into me,
these beats making me move so differently.
Swaying in memories
waiting to be made
of red ribbons strewn around you and me,
snow sprinkling down our windowpane,
and a full-track kiss of hot chocolate and peppermint on
tender lips.

WHEN YOU
TOOK MY HAND

You took my mittened hand in yours
one quiet Christmas Eve
and in that moment
I felt anew.
I felt complete and satisfied with you.
I wonder if you remember.
We walked these candy-color decorated and white-lit village
lanes.
Your dark blue glove enfolded my red,
the sound of chimes filled my ears,
and my heart fluttered in a natural response to it all being
unequivocally right.

The snow on our gloves glimmered.
The purest and sweetest happiness settled in my chest.
Beyond contentment,
a dream come true.
A gesture as simple as your hand enfolding mine
made millions of questioning moments disappear
into feeling chosen,
into feeling wanted.
This connection is incomparable, you know?
This unconditional love
you gave me,
took me so far away from the illusion I needed this touch from
another.
You showed me that had this been granted
with "him" or "him,"
this vulnerable moment—
my hand reaching out—
would have led to nothing but pinching self-loathing,
my heart only being exposed,
and me grappling with why I desired this so.
But never have I ever felt this disappointing possibility
with you.
And with you, I went back
to a time where I never questioned intimate moments could
be changed
to anything less than love.
And never will I again.
Through a simple awakening
in one moment
I took in this true feeling of everything I've always deserved
coming true.
When you took my hand in yours,
I found one true spark of all I'd ever need to know.

MY GROOVE

I play this song over and over again.
To you it's such a sad one.
The story doesn't turn out so well.
A man gave everything he had.
She left anyway.
Her heart belonged somewhere else.
You wonder why I love this track.
Tonight, I will tell you.
I have never . . .
No, not ever, been so in love!
This song has me diving deep,
into how very much I care for you.
I could never take losing you.

The wail of the steel guitar,
this melody with its still waters,
the real rasp in the singer's voice,
all these details have me reflecting,
how amazing it is to be with you.
All those butterflies start dancing in me,
and I think of all the simply sweet times
you've showed me,
how much I mean to you.
Three minutes and twenty-three seconds later,
I'm picking up the phone to call you.
Each and every night,
I'm telling you how very much I love you.
"I love you."
"There's no woman luckier than me."
"You've got me forever and always."

GONE

The ones who didn't value me,
those who smirked at my dreams,
saying she will wake up in time,
all who didn't show up,
all these people are gone,
because of the certainty you hold me with
on this dance floor tonight.
The palm of your left hand firmly on my waist
as I move with you
in my red dress.

Happy

There's a stirring
deep within me,
as pictures slide
into my heart's eyes
of all the blessings that have made me.
I feel the side-glance smiles,
sparkling eyes looking into mine,
dark skies illuminated with millions of lights,
walks through new cities,
and sweet clarity drives, in the midst of a confusion that could
have swallowed me whole.
It's you I see through it all,

my family,
behind every dream.

WEDDING BELLS

She hears a subtle chime,
steady and calm,
soft but clear
above the heart.
Her thoughts still waver on this wish,
to know a love with a specific kiss.
It's the kind of love that holds,
and is just the right amount of bold,
giving her this deep contentment
at this now complete home.
She still has her doubts,
but,

ding . . .
ding . . .
ding . . .
these bells play on,
closer to her center each time.

Unique Find

There was a light in your eyes,
when you saw me coming down the path.
There was a pattering in my heart,
when I felt the name of this love.
There was desire,
when we realized this deep simplicity is like catching magic.
From friends to lovers,
is where we began.

Authentically You

When a child needs you,
When an innocent needs you,
All walls come down.
Nothing stops you,
No prejudices,
No slights against you come into play,
You become

The person you were at the beginning of time.
You are
The person God created you to be,
Open and Free,
Your heart beating once again for all to see.

WHAT MEETS YOU

Elated,
Coming down
Into your lover's arms,
However temporary,
From one moment to another,
Until Kingdom and Everlasting Come.
Uncovering belief,
Treasure in these soul-soaked days and nights,
An all-encompassing heart's revelation,
This out-of-body energy does not die.
This supernatural earthly love is forever.

All of the authentically bright, will sail onward to the eternal
place.
There's a reason this place is called Heaven.
You don't take anything with you,
All that is golden meets you on the other side of the tunnel,
At the angel-welcoming white gates.

WITH EVERYTHING
YOU DO

With everything you do,
Please remember there may be someone looking up to you.

Maybe at this very moment.
Maybe somewhere in the future.
Maybe you will never know for sure.
But some moonlit evening,
Someone may be searching to uncover everything about you,
Inspired by stories or legends,
Or eyes that fell upon a footprint you made.
So please,
With everything you do,
Please remember,
There's a good chance,
Someone will want to look up to you.

My Violin

Hearing this violin after all the noise,
All the one-way talk,
Is comparative to finding the most sublime Heaven on Earth.
The way the music waltzes with each slide of the bow,
There's attention given to each and every note.
Listening into the depths of this far-from-hollow instrument,
Wanting to convey each and every piece,
Pure as a fresh spring,
The transcendent emotion played through,

Like breathing in Wyoming air,
And feeling the energy in a Long Island Summer,
Coming together in the prettiest song.
This is the sound of your love, for sure.
And I understand for the first time,
Never before,
Every little motion has led me here,
To this most gentle melody taking me in,
All heart,
And soul.

LITTLE BOY

Little Boy,
I pray for you to see what I see in you.
I see the brightest stars,
A spirit truly Heaven-Sent.
God broke the mold for sure.
He knew this cynical world needed your electric being.
I already see you as the saving grace to many hearts with the
sensitivity you hold,
If only given the chance.
The way your brown eyes light up when you smile,
My faith is expanded every time.
You are so young.

It has only been three years since you were dropped down
from above.
But I can see the way others are already beginning to label and
judge.
You're beautiful to me.
And that's why my wishes for you are as such.
I wish for you to have enormous strength in your heart,
With love always,
And the deeper understanding you will need.
Now I can fill you with all this belief,
But I wish for you to always have someone,
At least one someone
Telling you unmistakably,
Genuinely,
That you can't deny these truths when the clouds take over
your bright blue sky,
Your favorite color.
Little Boy,
I want you to always see yourself as remarkable,
The gift you truly are.
And to remember,
No matter how far away I may be,
There's someone who is cheering you on.
I believe in you.
There's a magic within I truly see.
You have already left a forever print on my heart,
Sweet Little Boy.

Snow Heart

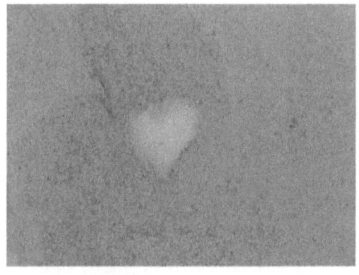

Stopped in her tracks
On a blustery February day—
"Do you see it?"
She asked him with joy flushed red on her face,
Pointing to a patch of snow on the beach that lay.
His eyes squinted,
Lips pursed,
He stood respectfully still,
In a moment of silence for what must be true to her.
"The snow, it's a heart!" she said with conviction,
Taking an instant picture
In fear that it may suddenly melt away.

He, knowing that she was a poetess, remarked
With equal conviction to her,
In his refreshingly sweet-to-her-ears accent,
"I think you see love everywhere."
If only he knew.
It was these signs, she believed, to be her saving grace,
Her purpose through healing writings she would forever
chase.

Not on My Own

It's said that you can only save yourself.

But then I imagine my life without the saxophone spinning those sharp notes,
The scatting and passionate plea way up high,
Speaking right to me it seems,
A message of, "you're going to pick yourself right back up again."

Then, a little child
No more than three
Runs to me,
Wrapping her little arms around me,
And I don't feel so breakable it seems.

And I recall what you said,
My friend,
One chilly night long ago.
"Your brown eyes light up the sky."
And it seems my own spirit, with sudden direction, takes flight,
With this remembrance never having left my soul.

THE WAY LIFE TURNS

When I was little, I secretly longed to break my arm. This may sound crazy to all of you adults now, but here lies my past reasoning:

All the girls who broke their bones had these great adventure stories to go along with their injury. Most of all they had neon bandages that many fans would leave black sharpie-written notes upon, wishing them well. Everyone, in a deeper sense, wanting to be a part of this person.

Never mind that if I had broken any bone, the store would have been sure to be out of the neon colors. Mom would have, of course, bought a pack of the prettiest neon sharpies and have come up with a creative covering all her own, but all of this wouldn't have changed my lack of popularity in those elementary school days.

No one would have asked to sign my arm. They may have asked how it happened in curiosity with a snotty tone, but they would not have stayed for the adventure story I had prepared specifically for their ears to go along with this broken arm.

I remember when I was little, I held inside how much I

wanted to be loved by just about everyone. I would hold doors and smile, hoping for a "thank you," a connection in another's eyes that would signal, "She's nice. I want to be friends with her!"

I sometimes wonder where those girls-turned-women who didn't give me the time of day are today. Are they the same? It's said that most people don't change.

I still hold doors and smile, always open to a connection in another's eyes.

Isn't life strange?

Now here I am tonight, on this stage signing book after book with a bright neon pink sharpie.

Unshakeable Heart

I must raise my hands up to my mom for this unshakeable
heart.
She encouraged me from the start.
Never to point at this way of being when heartbreak inevitably
threw its dart.
She always knew that what I felt was true.
Never fearful in the knowledge that our crew was few.
A reaching soul believes in the hope seen in the brightest
sunrise hue,
To restore even those living in the dullest state of blue.
Mom, you never discouraged this heart of mine,
Despite the exchange often not being a love that will bind.

Those touched may not even remember the expressions of
love.
The mix CD could have been thrown away years ago.
The album I created of shared pictures that meant everything
to me at one time.
Stories I wrote that documented my care for him.
All the letters.
I will never regret these actions I took,
This love I felt.

You encouraged me, Mom, to always love without conditions,
Through your example,
To follow what's yearning to be given to another.

This way of life has filled me with an abundant light that I use
on those darker days.

I honestly couldn't imagine surviving in this crazy world any
other way.

SCARLET

Standing for a love that does not fade,
Collecting kisses like heirloom ornaments,
All to recall on cloudy days that dreams do come true.
Reminders of what living is all about
Lest we lose ourselves along the way,
Every moment cherished like this is only the beginning of
forever,
Tomorrow even more exciting than today with the color of
scarlet in your soul.

LET IT BE ME

Let it be me who you run to when you see no way out.
Let it be me who you want to accompany you on thrilling
adventures.
Let it be me who brings you your favorite bright red straw-
berries,
And who bakes you your favorite cookies.
Let it be me who fills your soul when you need love the most,
The one who you tell all your deepest scars and dreams to.
Let it be me.

Oh please, let it be me,
Whose love you feel like no other.
Because I love you,
With every piece of me,
I do.

CHRISTMAS TIME

A frozen-lake sky.
The trees are bare.
At Christmas Time,
The saxophone seems to be heard everywhere.
It's a heart-on-your-sleeve,
Magical time of year.
With red garland and mistletoe coaxing me on,
My dreams are given their dare.
And it is with you,
At this Christmas Time that I know,
I can fearlessly go anywhere.

OUT OF THE BLUE

Out of the blue,
The story ahead suddenly widens and expands,
Though in the works all along.
The gift of what feels like a completely new life is finally here.
Glittered with innocence and heart from a small time in the
past.
What had been continually pushed back,
We are brought even more greatly, to who we individually are.
With a heart that keeps steadily but softly beating,
And a strong but thin thread of belief never splitting apart,
We can suddenly see that we've been designing each chapter all
along.

With the thrill of out-of-the-blue openings,
Your soul is finally free!
And anything is possible once again.
Out of the blue.

BEAUTIFUL GIRL

When you feel yourself going straight, I hope you know to make that turn.

Make time to run through a muddy field barefoot.

Remember how it feels, so you're pulled to do it more when life seems too restrictive.

Don't label experiences as "one time."

Remember that a kiss should never become routine.
Wear your hair down in the rain, especially.
Don't settle for less attention.
The little gestures do mean the most.
"Every day a surprise" is the way life is supposed to be.
It is all in how you view your days.
Don't forget to give love frequently and with your whole
heart.
You must constantly push yourself in achievement as well as in
restful contemplation.
Take time to reflect and mentally record your moments.
Don't let one achievement be your red light.
That's not what this life is all about.
Take in each day that you have been given.
Find the lesson, or peace, in every difficult circumstance you
face.
Don't let anyone ever break you down.
And I will try to do the same, in all of this advice I have
handed your way,
My Beautiful Girl.

OUR WINTER GETAWAY

Come along with me,
Down the glistening white-covered hill,
To our winter getaway.
Far from the city
But close to the village, with our favorite shops and galleries.

Let's snowshoe to our wood cabin house,
For it is the most fun to travel this way,
Through the land immersed in pine,
The cold nibbling at our faces,
Exhilarating our hearts!
"I'll race you!"

It turns out to be quite the tie.
Winner takes that long-held kiss!

We then open the door to the place we only dreamed of as
children.

Far from another home
But intimate with the place within, where our imaginations
continue to grow.

With nothing but romance and art on our minds,
We consider ourselves snowed-in.
A warm shower,
Our polished oak floors feeling smooth on our bare feet,
This place makes us free.

Oversized knit blankets keep us cozy,
With every warm light on.
I rest against your chest by the open fire.
And we toast to us with roasted marshmallows and Moët
Champagne
As the snow floats down outside our floor-to-ceiling window
panes.

Never Alone with Love

Dying alone—
People passively say we all do.
But I don't believe this has to be true.
So please pull me in close
And we will dance from room to room,
Your arms around me,
Full of genuine care.
I want to look into your eyes and see all that has led me here.
Like one of those photo-framed family trees,
Or like a slideshow showing
The moments we remember.
It's a story of giving and accepting what we all want the most,
What matters most.

For when I do find myself moving on to that eternal place,
I don't believe it's an end.
And I don't believe we will be alone.
My heart racing,
I will be dancing,
The same as now,
With you,
Feeling you holding me,
Me holding you,
Knowing I am defined by love.
Embracing now.
Embracing eternally.
Your hand reaching for mine on the other side.
I truly believe,
We will never be alone with love.

THAT SONG

You know that song that stops you in your tracks,
Has you aching for a plain old love,
Someone to kiss this instant,
Hold you tight,
Someone's eyes to look into, that tell you without words,
Everything is going to be alright because they will always be by
your side?

SECRET HIDEAWAY

A Caribbean Island,
Water often Misty Blue,
Where Pirate's Legends Reside
Back in My Childhood.

And This is Why I Love the Rain . . .

Pouring down,
The rain gives voice to emotions and truth.
Few see their raw hearts in the sunshine.
Relaying a message to slow down,
To care more,
To wake up before your life becomes something no longer lived,
I believe this is what the rain does.
I love the rain because it makes people look.
It often stops them in their tracks.
It makes them go deeply into their ignored heart.
Inspiration strikes in the quiet, simply listening to the rain fall.

Maybe it makes some people sad.
I think that is good.
For change only occurs when straying from the norm.
Cleansing the earth and the sky,
The rain is a new beginning if you open your eyes.
I love the rain!
"Let it pour!" I say with a grateful soul on this stormy Sunday
morning.

Bringing Back Life

When we were little,
We palmed the bark of trees when playing tag,
And dug in the dirt for buried treasure.
The sparkling pebbles and stones we'd find,
The scent of warm fresh air and earth,
We collected leaves,
We collected seashells,
We melded our hands into the wet sand
On the edge between ocean and shoreline.
Catching lightning bugs at night,
Watching them fly and glow yellow as we set them free,
Under the black sky with the moon and stars.

The labor and zest for life, rolling a snowball in the cold
nipping winter,
Touching formed icicles like fine crystal,
Such beauty and belief were stirred.
And these natural acts as a child haven't gone away, you see?
Nature is waiting for us to recapture it all,
To reignite all that we have always been a part of.
Our childhood is not gone,
It is only waiting for us to once again, with our hearts, see.

Alive

Alive
Like the heaviest hurt having been lifted,

Alive
As the electric guitar encapsulating the depth and overcoming
elements of a great story,
Alive
Like a love first experienced,
Alive
As a two in the morning road trip start,
Alive
Like the first rays of summer,
Alive
As your life's ribbon begins to be seen poetically and followed
with renewed faith.

BLESSED

How wonderful it is TO YEARN,
For that musical-like dance with your one true love.
The first sight of your "heart work" lifting others.
For all your deepest dreams to come true.

How lovely it is TO SEE,
The beautiful smiles that surround you every day.
The bright green leaves on a bamboo growing higher.
A young child running wildly free.

How remarkable it is TO HEAR,
A new song that reaches right into your soul.

"My life is complete with you."
The energy of waves crashing against the shore.

How captivating it is TO FEEL,
All this life.
A life that you know belongs to you.
All this love times two.

YOUR CITY

Your home.
I want to see,
The details that still hold,
Secret places filled with your prints.
Show me.

Adventure List

There are so many places she wants to go.
She never cared for the term "Bucket List."
The name strikes her as blasé and callous for a life we are only
given one.
She prefers an "Adventure List" that will continue to grow
long after this poem is written.
She pictures:
Seeing the zebras and elephants in Zimbabwe.
The flamingos on Lake Naivasha.
Hiking through the valley of Lauterbrunnental, Switzerland
to stand before the waterfalls.
Exploring the Emerald Isle of Ireland with her mom.

Traveling on the classic and elegant Orient Express with her brother.

Honeymooning in the Tahitian Islands.

And all these trips and more to be taken through the lens of extraordinary, blessed love of every kind!

ENCORE

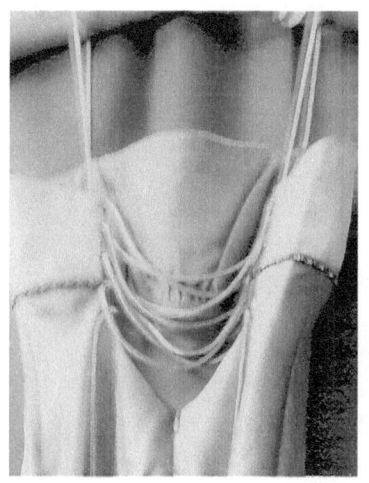

Inside of me plays R & B.
Inside of you, similar I see.

I crave your caress,
On this scarlet, silver-sparkled slip dress.

Let the electric guitar pull every chord tonight,
The high vocal notes making the notion of tomorrow out of
sight.

I need to be free,
You seeing every facet of me.

The two of us to shine bright,
This unhindered love taking off like an unstrung kite.

Acknowledgments

Thank you to all of my loved ones, as always, and to all those in my past who have led me to where I am today through love or lessons—I am grateful for you all and that is why I will always say that there is not a single person in this world who is "self-made." My soul has been shaped by everyone who has entered my life, and is expanded by my dreams and the people and experiences still to come.

Thank you to God for this love of music and writing that I have, and for a soulful heart that pangs with a desire to turn even the difficult times into something beautiful.

I would also like to thank Harbor Lane Books for bringing these poetry collections of mine to you all, and for continually believing in my art.

About the Author

Christie Leigh Babirad lives on Long Island and is a poetess of numerous collections. She continually aspires to illuminate the moments in life, no matter the size or subject, and create art that will not fade with the passing time.

You can follow her work on social media at the following sites to find out more about her latest projects.

facebook.com/authorchristieleighbabirad

instagram.com/christieleighbabiradauthor

youtube.com/@christieleighbabirad1707

goodreads.com/cbabiradauthor

ABOUT THE PUBLISHER

Harbor Lane Books, LLC is a US-based independent digital publisher of commercial fiction, non-fiction, and poetry.

Connect with Harbor Lane Books on their website (www. harborlanebooks.com) and social media @harborlanebooks.

facebook.com/harborlanebooks

x.com/harborlanebooks

instagram.com/harborlanebooks

tiktok.com/@harborlanebooks

threads.com/harborlanebooks

pinterest.com/harborlanebooks

Evergreen
poems

CHRISTIE LEIGH BABIRAD

Lilacs
and
Roses

A POETRY COLLECTION

CHERYL BABIRAD
CHRISTIE LEIGH BABIRAD

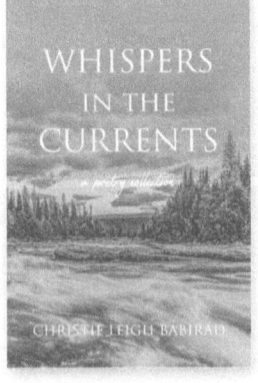

WHISPERS
IN THE
CURRENTS

a poetry reflection

CHRISTIE LEIGH BABIRAD

WHISPERS
IN THE
VELVET BLUE

a poetry collection

CHRISTIE LEIGH BABIRAD

www.ingramcontent.com/pod-product-compliance
Lightning Source LLC
Chambersburg PA
CBHW020232130626
46549CB00005B/1855